0

1 **blue**

0

0

3 **green**

0

yellow

5 **orange**

1

2

0

3

9 **three**

4

0

5

0

6

0

0

0

0

0

0

0

1

1

1

29 **man**

1

1

1

1

33 **mum**

1

2

2

2

Hello

2

 bookcase

2

2

2

 watermelon

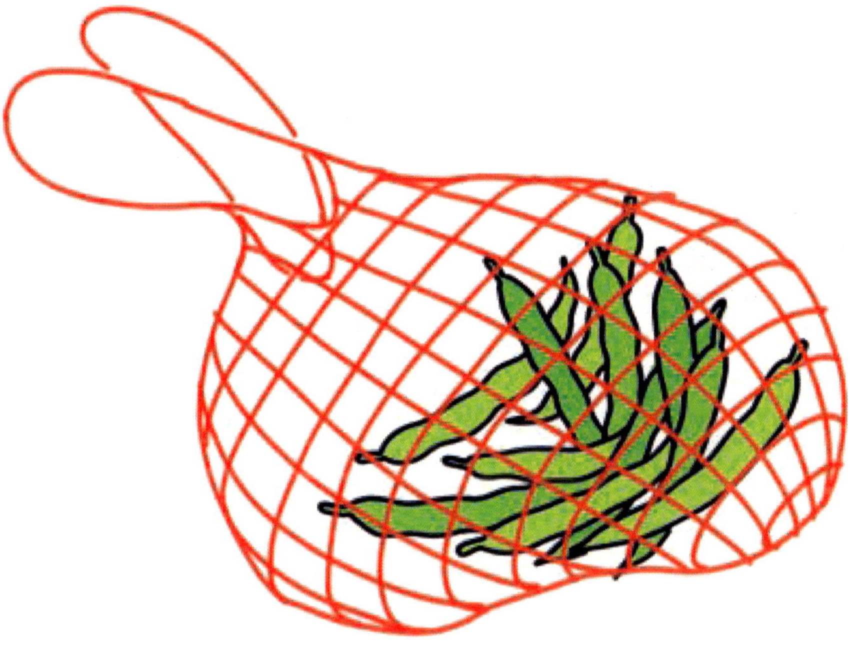

 burger

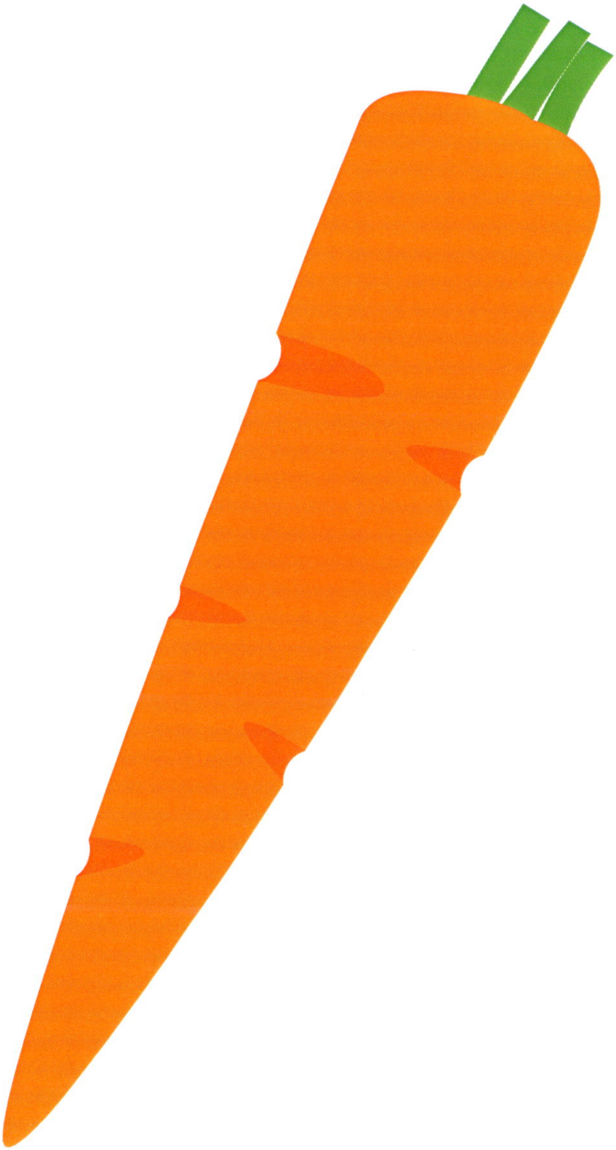

3

4

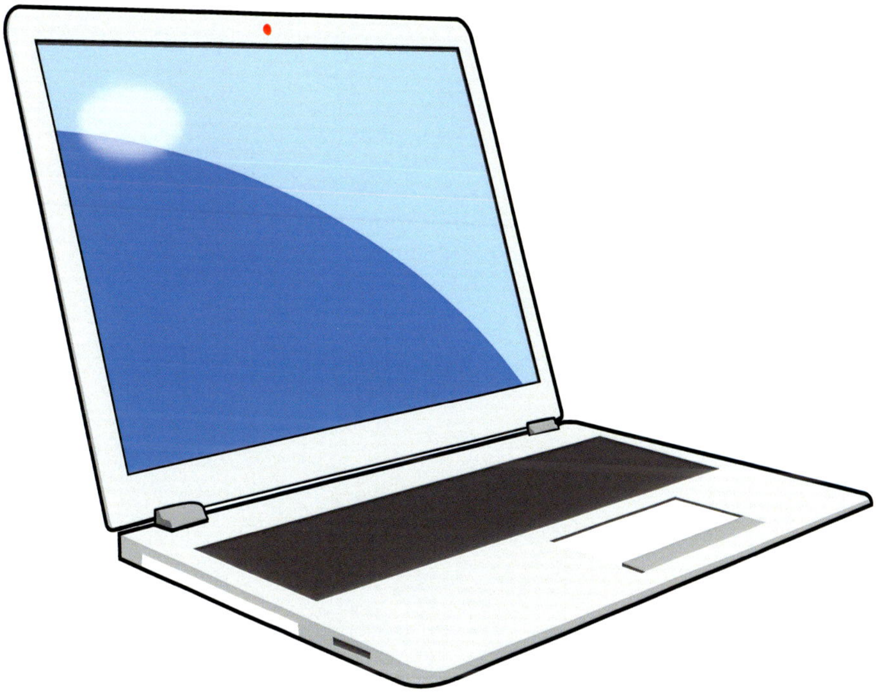

4

5

5

5

5

69 **mouth**

5

5

5

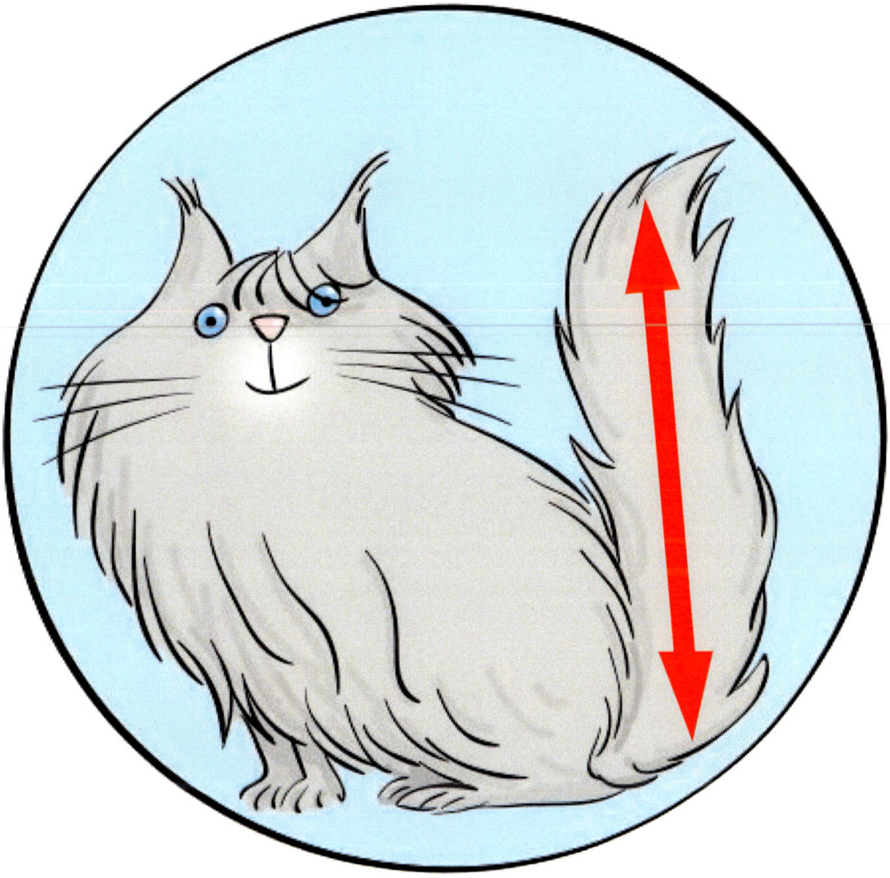

5

5

6

6

ball

6

6

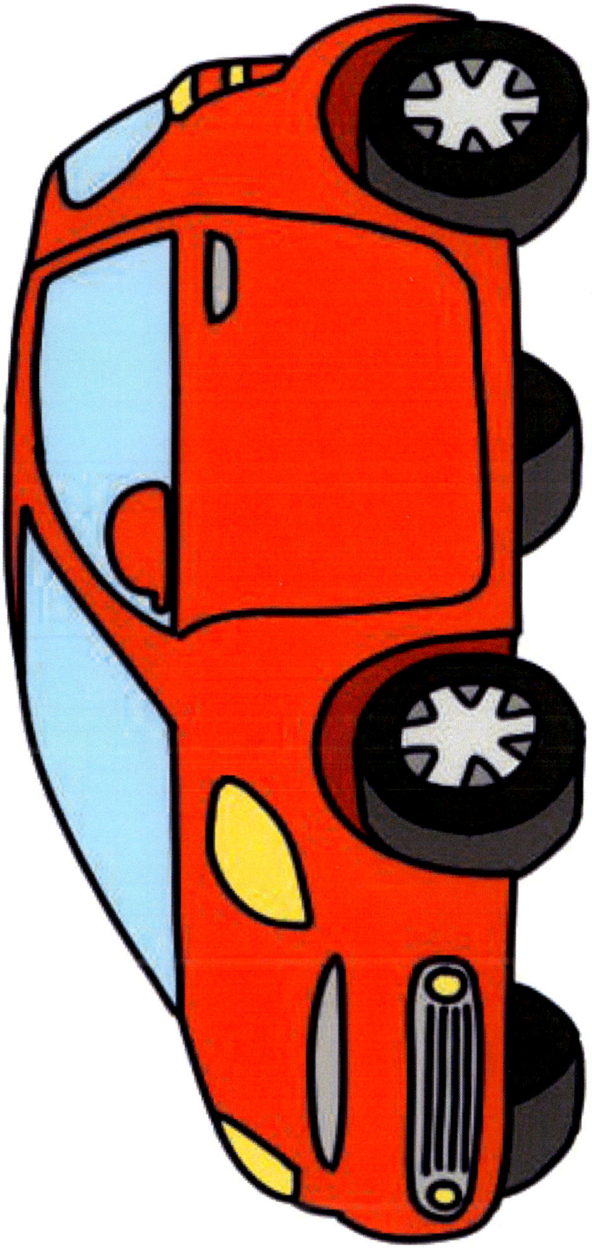

6

climb

87 **jump**

7

 swim

7

90 **walk**

7

7

 play basketball

7

 play the piano

8

8

 take a photo

8

9

 jeans

9

9

9

9

 sheep